NET NEUTRALITY FOR BROADBAND:

UNDERSTANDING THE FCC'S 2015 OPEN INTERNET ORDER

AND OTHER ESSAYS

MATTHEW HOWARD

Net Neutrality for Broadband: Understanding the FCC's 2015 Open Internet Order and Other Essays.

Paperback ISBN 10: 0692594566
Paperback ISBN 13: 978-0692594568
Kindle Ebook ASIN: B0190KLGJE

CONTENTS

PREFACE

Net neutrality started out contentious and only became more so. The first essay in this booklet traces the technology and policy developments which led to the 2015 Open Internet Order, the FCC regulation which formalized many aspects of what we consider a neutral net. Originally published in December 2015, this essay brought readers up to speed on the policy's history, meaning, and legal implications.

But in the ever-changing world of public policy, nothing stays the same for very long. By the time February 2017 rolled around, readers were overdue for a comprehensive update on the saga of the 2015 Order. You will find it in the third essay now included in this booklet: *Two Years of Net Neutrality*. It updates pending court decisions from the 2015 essay, reviews the legal actions the FCC used to enforce the Order's provisions, and addresses the FCC's leadership changes following the 2016 presidential election.

Throughout 2017, my policy writing focused on a related topic: municipal broadband networks. But all year long, the debate about net neutrality continued to rage, and the fate of the 2015 Order is now more uncertain than ever.

My goal is to take challenging policy topics and make them accessible to general readers, while maintaining the depth of research and analysis expected from academic works. If these essays give you a clear picture of where net neutrality has been, where it is now, and where it may head in the future, then I have succeeded.

But like you, I'm very curious to see what happens next. We have not yet reached the end of the road with net neutrality, but major changes may be just around the corner.

Net Neutrality for Broadband:
Understanding the FCC's 2015 Open Internet Order

I. Introduction.

The Federal Communications Commission's 2015 Open Internet Order, championed as a major advance in establishing net neutrality, reclassifies broadband Internet access as a common carriage telecommunication service rather than an information service. The agency's new classification brings broadband under the Title II authority of the Telecommunications Act of 1996. Why is this such an important move for the FCC?

To begin with, the Telecommunications Act of 1996 did not foresee technologies converging. It failed to anticipate that future emerging technologies would bring competing services onto different physical networks than the ones traditionally associated with them. This resulted in numerous, lengthy court cases where judges had to puzzle over such questions as whether the FCC has Title VI authority to regulate streaming video over the internet like it does with multichannel video programming, or if the FCC has Title II authority to regulate Voice over IP services on broadband like it does with traditional wireline telephony. Or does any service provided over the Internet fall under the incredibly vague authority given in Title I? Lawyers argued these points for years, but nobody knew for sure, and consensus was hard to come by.

With such matters tied up in the courts, it is no wonder that regulation had completely failed to keep up with the engineering realities of Internet technology. The new Title II classification of broadband as a telecommunications service has the potential to eliminate this litigious waste of time and resources by clearly defining the FCC's authority and allowing the agency to move forward. The reclassification also brings regulatory authority into a more realistic alignment with technology. Just as technology has converged, regulation is converging. Rather than having all these services spread out into separate Titles, they now converge into one: Title II.

Though the reclassification rode a wave of popular and political support, it is not without its detractors. The 2015 Open Internet Order, opposed by many corporate interests in the Internet industry, faces potential legislative and judicial challenges. In seeking to resolve longstanding questions, the Order brings its own battery of economic and engineering difficulties in a time when the FCC seeks to promote expansion of broadband nationwide, even into traditionally underserved and rural communities. This essay will affirm the FCC's decision and its intended benefits, summarize the technological and legal background leading up to it, and highlight the significant political and technological challenges which remain to be solved.

II. TECHNOLOGICAL BACKGROUND OF CLASSIFYING BROADBAND.

The technical aspects summarized in this section receive a more detailed, historical analysis in the book *Digital Crossroads: Telecommunications Law and Policy in the Internet Age* by Jonathan E. Nuechterlein and Philip J. Weiser, especially chapters 1, 2 and 5. (See the Annotated Bibliography.)

From Waves to Digits. The problem of regulating Internet access, and the question of the FCC's scope of authority in doing so, began with the technology that made it all possible: digital encoding of information. When information began to go digital, telecommunication was an analog industry. From vinyl records to telephone signals, communication relied on creating physical and electrical analogs of sound waves (or, as in photography and other visual media, light waves). From the physical grooves in a vinyl record to the electromagnetic waves which power speakers and amplifiers, information was re-created in a physical form analogous to the information source.

Digital technology changed all that. Digital technology sampled the information source, numerous times per second, and broke that sample down into a binary code: a string of ones and zeroes. The two binary digits communicated a state to transistors: on or off, open or closed. Transmitting these digital samples created the world of packets, where the encoded information would be broken down into smaller pieces. Each packet contained additional code which identified what larger group it belonged to, and where it belonged in the sequence of samples. The signal's receiver would reassemble all the packets in the correct order according to this additional information in the packet headers.

A Binary Journey. This method came with certain challenges for transmitting information "live" or in "real time". The receiver might put the packets together out of order, a phenomenon known as jitter. Or it might take different packets different lengths of time to arrive at the receiver, creating a waiting period known as latency (or, more commonly, "lag"). Advances in digital technology eventually solved much of these problems. However, they are important to keep in mind when understanding some of the arguments against net neutrality and the 2015 Open Internet Order.

To ensure that packets would not take too long to travel from transmitter to receiver, Internet networks and service or content providers developed paid prioritization. For example, a provider of videoconferencing services would want to avoid latency and delays in the signals for a conference, wanting instead for the users to have a smooth, uninterrupted service. So, the provider would pay the networks to prioritize the relevant packets. It seemed like a good solution, and still does to a great number of companies in the digital information industry. After all, packets conveying an email message or a text-only web page do not need to be constantly transmitted "live". Those can be sent one time, and super-fast speed is not so important to the user's receipt and enjoyment of the signal. Paid prioritization became a way for providers to ensure a reasonably high quality of service for urgent signals, and for networks to have a financial incentive to make that possible. The FCC's declaring an end to these paid prioritization agreements remains a contentious aspect of the 2015 Open Internet Order.

The Rise of Cable and Dial-up. The Order's reclassifying Internet access as a telecommunications service has also garnered many objections. So, it helps to understand the technological background underlying this dispute. Broadband Internet access, though now possible through both physical cables and wireless radio waves, began with the rise of cable television. Cable TV companies competed with the older television networks by building a massive infrastructure to run coaxial cable directly to people's residences. This robust cable network could provide more bandwidth and a more reliable signal than the existing radio wave networks. Eventually, these cable companies began to maximize those advantages by offering Internet access, too.

But before that happened, Internet access took place using the existing infrastructure of the telephone companies. To access the Internet, a user connected a computer modem to a phone line and dialed up an Internet service provider on the same network they would use to place a phone call. This dial-up technology gave rise to one of the fundamental problems of definition that has plagued regulators for roughly twenty years.

The Convergence. The FCC had developed regulatory approaches to the existing copper-wire telephone networks, and telephony was seen as a distinctly different service than the digital information service provided by the Internet. Telecommunications generally meant telephone service, and its regulation focused on restraining the monopolistic power of the phone companies: first, AT&T with its massive nationwide network which enabled long-distance calls, and later the Bell companies formed by splitting up AT&T into smaller companies which provided primarily local telephone service. Because the Internet spawned the birth of companies not related to AT&T and the Bells, and because its digital data processing capabilities bore little resemblance to analog phone service, the FCC saw telephony and Internet as two very separate things.

However, one can easily see the problem of treating Internet access differently when it is accessed using the very same physical infrastructure as telephone service thanks to dial-up technology. As technologies began to converge, "telephone" calls became possible over the new digital and cable networks. Treating these services differently became increasingly problematic. The Internet eventually made it possible to use the same infrastructure and networks to access data processing and information services, participate in voice communication, receive video content and music, and any form of information which could be digitally sampled and encoded. Technology had at last converged. But, as we shall see, regulation experienced its own difficult form of latency, lagging far behind this technological convergence. The problems thus created are problems the 2015 Open Internet Order seeks to resolve.

III. LEGAL BACKGROUND OF CLASSIFYING BROADBAND.

The Telecommunications Act of 1996. In 1996, Congress updated an Act from 1934, the same Act which created the FCC and laid the foundation for the agency's authority. At that time, the FCC's major concerns included encouraging the interstate telephone network to become a truly universal service for all citizens, not simply by expanding networks but by keeping prices for residential customers low (Nuechterlein, 2013, p. 38). The FCC focused on encouraging competition in the telecommunications industry by removing barriers to entry for new companies (ibid, p. 52). As part of achieving these goals, the FCC required nondiscrimination in both pricing and services. A telephone company could charge for its service or charge to lease its network capacity and facilities. But it could not give preferential pricing to different parties for those things.

The FCC's authority to make these requirements came from certain sections of the Communications Act known together as Title II (Jacobs, 2015, p. 1). Title II set forth the FCC's scope of powers to regulate telephony as a common carriage service (Nuechterlein, 2013, p. 21). "Generally, common carriage refers to a requirement that all customers be offered service on a standardized and non-discriminatory basis, and may include a requirement that those services be priced reasonably" (Ruane, 2014, p. 12).

But by 1996, new technologies had arrived, including the Internet. The updated Act distinguished between traditional telephony (a telecommunications service) and information services, placing the latter not under Title II but under Title I (Signaigo, 2007, p. 2). Title I did not have the same common carriage aspects as Title II (ibid). In fact, Title I gave the FCC "little specific jurisdictional guidance"

(Ohlhausen, 2015, p. 208). With its authority to regulate Title I information services so vaguely defined, the FCC invoked a similarly vague "ancillary authority" in this area (Nuechterlein, 2013, p. 232). This unfortunate state of affairs resulted in much debate in the courts when the FCC attempted to regulate information services, including Internet access.

But the Title I classification of Internet access had more problems than ill-defined regulatory authority. It also suffered from an acute lack of foresight into the Internet's emerging technology. It failed to foresee a world where convergence would blur the distinctions between telecommunications and the types of data processing which fell under the information services classification (ibid, p. 231). The 1996 Act, coming into effect just as email, web sites, and search engines were becoming fully integrated into daily life, quickly became obsolete in its treatment of Internet regulation. Splitting voice, video, and information into separate Titles began to make little sense. "With the convergence of various technologies—for instance, Voice over Internet Protocol (VoIP) competing with circuit-switched telephony or Internet Protocol Television (IPTV) competing with broadcast and cable—this siloed approach to regulation is increasingly out of step with reality" (Ohlhausen, 2015, p. 208). The difference between the various Titles rapidly became increasingly irrelevant to a world where voice, video, audio, and text could all be digitally encoded and served over the Internet.

The Judicial Battleground. In the wake of this sorely flawed legislation, the FCC's attempts to regulate aspects of the Internet typically met with litigation. Federal courts would be asked to interpret the scope of the FCC's authority based on the law as provided by the Act. Was a regulatory measure within the FCC's scope of power? Had the FCC correctly interpreted the classification of telecommunication service versus information service?

Was the agency's regulation allowable under Title I or Title II? Just what does "ancillary authority" mean?

These questions required judges to sort through incredibly complex engineering and economic arguments which would have more easily been settled by clear and realistic legislative guidelines. But with only the inadequate wording of the 1996 Act to guide them, judges found themselves struggling to craft logical and meaningful interpretations. They also found themselves in disagreement, as differences of opinion between State, Circuit, and the Supreme Courts revealed, as well as the number of dissenting opinions which revealed a lack of consensus about these matters even within a single court. In short, "the legislature, the courts, and the FCC have all grappled with definitions, and the results have been generally confusing and inconsistent" (Signaigo, 2007, p. 1). At the heart of many of these judicial battles lay the question of whether or not the Internet was a telecommunication service or an information service, and therefore if it would fall under Title II or Title I, respectively. This debate came to a head in the *Brand X* case.

The *Brand X* Decision. A simplistic understanding of *Brand X* would lead one to believe the Supreme Court had ruled broadband Internet access was an information service, in agreement with the FCC's classification at that time. However, the Supreme Court opinion merely recognizes this classification was a *reasonable* interpretation on the FCC's part, even if it was not the *best* or *only* interpretation. The opinion argues that, due to the vague wording of the 1996 Act, it is entirely within the FCC's authority as a federal agency to make its own reasonable interpretation.

"If a statute is ambiguous, and if the implementing agency's construction is reasonable, *Chevron* requires a federal court to accept the agency's construction of the statute, even if the agency's reading differs from what the court believes is the best statutory interpretation" (p. 8).

The majority opinion found the classification reasonable, but the dissenting opinion by Justice Scalia expresses animosity towards it. The majority accepted arguments that the telecommunications hardware involved was an inseparable part of the tools to access the service, a service which could be understood as information service. Therefore, the majority reasoned, the hardware did not necessarily change the underlying nature of the service. Scalia's dissent argued against this reasoning, asserting that the use of telecommunications hardware was an obvious use of telecommunication service, and that divorcing the service and the access network into two types of classifications made no practical sense. This dissent agreed with the lower court which had decided that broadband access was clearly a telecommunication service and could not legitimately be regulated as anything but. The majority handled this logic by making it clear it was not up to the courts to decide the classification, per the *Chevron* precedence. It was, in the majority's opinion, the responsibility of the FCC to make the classification, and courts should uphold the FCC decision even if they did not agree with it, as long as the decision was reasonable.

This case makes two things clear. First, the courts have a major problem finding consensus on a law that arbitrarily splits telecommunication and information into two different things. It is a split which defies logic and therefore makes logical, consistent conclusions nearly impossible. As one analysis of the Brand X case summarizes it,

"The difficulty that the FCC and the courts have had with shoehorning modern technologies into the FCC classifications simply underscores the need for change or even elimination of these classifications.

Distinguishing between 'basic' telecommunications service and 'enhanced' information services no longer makes sense in light of the complexity of these technologies" (Signaigo, 2007, p. 395).

Second, the responsibility and authority to choose how the Internet is classified rests not with the courts but with the FCC. The *Brand X* decision holds that the FCC may, under current law, decide whether or not broadband Internet is a telecommunication service or an information service. The FCC's interpretation of *Brand X* agrees with this analysis. As Section C.43 of the 2015 Order puts it,

"Exercising our delegated authority to interpret ambiguous terms in the Communications Act, as confirmed by the Supreme Court in *Brand X*, today's Order concludes that the facts in the market today are very different from the facts that supported the Commission's 2002 decision to treat cable broadband as an information service" (FCC, 2015, Feb. 26, p. 14).

Therefore, when opponents of the 2015 Open Internet Order argue that the FCC has no authority to reclassify broadband under Title II as a telecommunication service, they betray a shallow understanding of the *Brand X* decision. The FCC may have classified broadband one way for years, but that classification is theirs to make—or, as is now the case, to remake.

IV. POPULAR AND POLITICAL PRESSURES FOR NET NEUTRALITY.

Popular Pressure. The FCC's exercise of its authority to reclassify broadband, however, did not take place without pressures from inside and outside the agency. Aside from being a solution to recurring legal difficulties, it was a response to popular pressure. As FCC Chairman Tom Wheeler would state when the 2015 Order was announced,

> "We heard from startups and world-leading tech companies. We heard from ISPs, large and small. We heard from public-interest groups and public-policy think tanks. We heard from Members of Congress, and, yes, the President. Most importantly, we heard from nearly 4 million Americans who overwhelmingly spoke up in favor of preserving a free and open Internet" (FCC, 2015, p.1).

This overwhelming support, however, was not unanimous. As *The Wall Street Journal* reported, "more than 100 Internet companies" including Amazon, Google, and Facebook united to send Wheeler a letter that his plans would threaten the Internet, not benefit it (Nagesh, 2014). Nevertheless, Internet communities such as Reddit would champion the cause, at one time "making over 15,000 calls in a span of just three hours" to the FCC and congressional representatives (Alexis, 2015). In April 2014, Josh Levy of Free Press joined with David Segal (Demand Progress), Amalia Deloney (Center for Media Justice), Sarah Morris (Open Technology Institute) and first-amendment lawyer Marvin Ammori to host a Reddit discussion forum, explain what was at stake with net neutrality, and urge users to get politically involved by contacting their representatives and the FCC directly (Levy, 2014). What was the result of these digital grass-roots campaigns? By September 2014, *The Washington Post* reported the FCC had received a record-breaking 3 million comments on net neutrality (Fung, 2014).

Presidential Pressure. If popular movements built pressure from the bottom, the executive branch applied pressure from the top. As the ACLU reported in *Network Neutrality 101*, the Bush-era FCC's classification of broadband as an information service, exempt from common carriage requirements, was challenged in the Supreme Court, but the Court deferred to the FCC and allowed the exemption (Stanley, 2010, p. 14). Events would take a different course following the end of the Bush presidency, though the FCC's vote on the 2015 Order split along party lines, with Republicans against it and Democrats for it.

In a shift from the previous presidential stance, President Barack Obama voiced support for the idea of a free and open internet, lending credence to the FCC's efforts. In November 2014, President Obama urged the FCC "to adopt the 'strongest possible rules' on net neutrality", specifically including the classification of "high-speed broadband service as a utility under Title II" (Ruiz, 2015). *The New York Times* quoted President Obama as saying, "For most Americans, the Internet has become an essential part of everyday communication and everyday life" (ibid). The idea that the Internet has become such an integral part of daily American life, to the same extent that other utilities like electricity and running water have, bolsters the idea that it should be regulated as such. It has become, for many, a necessity rather than a luxury good.

But President Obama's influence on the 2015 Order began much earlier. He furthered this reclassification agenda when he nominated businessman and former communications industry lobbyist Tom Wheeler to the FCC in May 2013 (White House, 2013). Less than a year later, Wheeler would assume the position of Chairman.

Internal Pressure. Tom Wheeler's becoming the FCC Chairman in November 2013, marks a major turning point in the net neutrality saga. Wheeler joined the FCC at a time when, within the agency, the idea of net neutrality had been gaining traction but failed to become fully realized. FCC efforts to promote net neutrality go back to 2005, when then-Chairman Kevin J. Martin spearheaded a policy statement about "Four Internet Freedoms" users were entitled to, including "access to any lawful content", and "benefit from competition among network providers" (Stanley, 2010, p. 16). This Internet Policy Statement was more an idea than an enforceable act. Although "the FCC maintained that it had sufficient authority to enforce the principles", the Statement "was not promulgated into regulation" (Ruane, 2014, p. 1). In fact, Comcast fought for its right to discriminate against certain forms of data in *Comcast vs. FCC*, and won the battle in the DC Circuit Court in 2010 (Stanley, 2010, p. 16).

The FCC tried again with the 2010 Open Internet Order. It attempted many of the same things the 2015 Order would set forth, but it faced a major problem. With broadband Internet access still classified as a Title I information service rather than a Title II telecommunication service, some aspects of the Order fell outside of the FCC's established authority. This explains the DC Circuit Court's 2014 decision, in *Verizon v. FCC*, to strike down the blocking and antidiscrimination provisions. The Court saw these provisions, though not the disclosure requirements, as imposing common carriage requirements on a non-telecommunication service (Jacobs, 2014, p. 1). In hindsight, it was the FCC's own classification scheme that made the 2010 Order lack teeth. Writing for the majority, Circuit Court Judge Tatel said,

> "We think it obvious that the Commission would violate the Communications Act were it to regulate broadband providers as common carriers. Given the Commission's still-binding decision to classify broadband providers not as providers of 'telecommunications services' but instead as providers of 'information services'... such treatment would run afoul of section 153(51): 'A telecommunications carrier shall be treated as a common carrier under this [Act] only to the extent that it is engaged in providing telecommunications services'" (Tatel, 2014, p. 45).

But alongside net neutrality, Chairman Wheeler also promoted the idea of broadband expansion on a national level, to bring high-speed Internet connections to underserved and rural areas. It makes sense to view these two priorities as two prongs of the same policy goal. Wheeler desires not only to make broadband a universal service for all citizens, but also to guarantee that service would provide unimpeded access to information on a nondiscriminatory, freely flowing basis.

Under the information service classification, broadband providers stood to create an even greater gap in the so-called digital divide between rich and poor, dividing internet access into "pay-to-play fast lanes for Internet and media companies that can afford it, and slow lanes for everyone else" (Ruiz, 2015). They could also act as censors, deciding what content their subscribers could access. This is no theoretical proposition, but one specifically argued for by plaintiffs in the 2015 case *United States Telecom Association v. FCC* who wish to block content they find objectionable. We shall look at this case in greater detail later.

Reclassifying broadband under Title II authority was the right policy move to achieve the FCC's goals. It would both eliminate the legal and litigation problems stemming from the vagueness of the 1996 Act, and clarify the FCC's authority to keep the ever-expanding broadband networks aligned with the populist goals of a free and open Internet. The complex prioritization schemes and companies' ability to effectively censor the Internet through throttling and blocking had no place in the future envisioned by Chairman Wheeler and his supporters. The 2015 Open Internet Order aimed to secure the FCC's authority to guide the industry into this future.

V. Contentious Requirements of the 2015 Open Internet Order.

Clarifying Authority and Redefining Broadband. As we have seen, the FCC's vague Title I authority over information services has resulted in difficult legal battles and undermined its efforts to encourage broadband expansion. We need not reiterate the reclassification's significance here. But two points about this classification should be made before examining other aspects of the Order.

First, the FCC has decided to refrain or "forebear" from "enforcing provisions of Title II that are not relevant to modern broadband service", requirements normally faced by common carriage telecommunications service (FCC, 2015, Feb. 4). Many of these requirements developed in an age where the old copper-wire telephone network reigned supreme. Regulation evolved in the specific context of fostering competition in the telephone industry, seeking to restrain the monopolistic power of AT&T and its offspring the Bell companies, while simultaneously encouraging the entry of new companies into the market to spur innovation and keep prices low. Therefore, it would make little sense to suddenly subject all the existing broadband networks to provisions which were never intended to address their infrastructures, technologies, corporate structures, and competitive realities. (A complete table of these forbearances appears in *Highlights of the 2015 Open Internet Order*, pages 5-8. See Jacobs, Annotated Bibliography.)

Second, the Order treats broadband as having a download speed of 25Mbps or higher. This definition stems from the FCC's 2015 Broadband Progress Report (Singleton, 2015). Could this definition prove problematic? It seems, at first glance, the FCC has left a vast field of Internet service under the old classification, purely on the basis of speed. It makes little sense to define a connection speed of 24Mbps (or less) one way, and the same service (only faster) another way.

However, this problem is less about definition and more about focus. The FCC would like to see broadband access on a nationwide basis, and will push towards that future. In a 2014 hearing before the U.S. House Committee on Small Business, Chairman Wheeler made it clear that he did not consider 4Mbps fast enough at all, and he objected to subsidizing what he considered a sub-par speed (Brodkin, 2014). Therefore, Wheeler's FCC has chosen to focus on what may well become the new industry standard. As technology continues to increase bandwidth, we can anticipate the market will demand it. An internet connection of 25Mbps is already available from many cable providers, and even the wireless industry is looking to build more robust networks at that speed. AT&T recently announced a wireless broadband initiative intended to deliver speeds of 15Mbps to 25Mbps without relying on fixed-line cable infrastructure (Reed, 2015). Initiatives such as this may well serve Chairman Wheeler's intention of seeing broadband access for the entire nation. The FCC has chosen a forward-thinking definition of broadband so it may focus on these emerging technological advancements.

Service Requirements versus Free Speech Arguments. The 2015 Order deals with more than just the reclassification. It contains requirements aligned with the idea of net neutrality and the open exchange of information on the Internet. These include prohibitions against blocking any lawful content or unreasonably interfering with data transmission. These prohibitions seek to prevent Internet service providers from choosing what websites users may view on their network, and from throttling data from websites the ISP might not want to transmit. These prohibitions are bolstered with rules against impairing or degrading access to the Internet. These rules support a neutral net from the perspective of the information users can access unimpeded. The FCC also considered users by creating rules about mandatory disclosures aimed at making network management more transparent.

But these rules have met with an unexpected legal backlash. While advocates for "free speech" have long championed the net neutrality cause, members of the private, corporate sector have attempted to use free speech as an argument *against* the 2015 Order. In the words of Fred Campbell, executive director for the Center for Boundless Innovation in Technology, "A total ban on the editorial discretion of Internet service providers violates the First Amendment's command that Congress shall make no law abridging the freedom of the press" (Court Plans Speedy Review, 2015, p. 7). Campbell seems oblivious to the fact that the FCC is not Congress, and he confuses the FCC's prohibition against censorship with "leaving nothing to stop government censorship" of Internet speech (ibid).

But Campbell is not alone in making this duplicitous argument. Alamo Broadband, in a Joint Petition in a case involving the United States Telecom Association, asked the Court to review the FCC's 2015 Open Internet Order. The petitioners object to the Order on the grounds that 1) the Order's prohibition of blocking Internet content violates First Amendment "free speech" rights, 2) Section 706 of the Telecommunications Act does not authorize the kind of rules the Order creates, and 3) Sections 201(b) and 303(b) of the Act do not authorize the prohibition of paid prioritization agreements (Joint Brief, 2015, p. 12). The petitioners claim broadband providers "engage in speech" and exercise "editorial discretion" in deciding "which speech to transmit" (Joint Brief, 2015, p. 13). One might ask, "Which is it?" Is an ISP speaking, or is it transmitting speech?

The FCC responded that broadband providers are transmitters of other speakers, not speakers themselves, and this seems logically correct. The FCC's Brief in this case draws a clear distinction between subscribing to information sources such as *The Wall Street Journal*, which people recognize as a provider of *content*, and ordering broadband access from a cable company, which people understand as a "transmission service that supplies *access* to... content" (Brief, 2015, p. 24-25). The FCC's Brief points out that "Verizon's operation of *Huffington Post*, for example, is left untouched" because the FCC is not regulating content or speech (ibid, p. 25). Instead, the 2015 Order means subscribers to Verizon's *broadband* services will not have their access to other content blocked, regardless of whether or not Verizon owns such content providers or sanctions their views.

The petitioners further argue that their own First Amendment rights are violated because the FCC's anti-blocking rules "compel providers to carry all speech, including political speech with which providers disagree" (Joint Brief, 2015, p. 13). The petitioners wish to engage in blocking content with political views they find objectionable. In other words, the petitioners envision "free speech" as a state of affairs where they can block the speech of others, and object to the FCC's order to freely transmit all forms of lawful speech. The petitioners have turned the idea of "free speech" on its head by arguing that the First Amendment protects their ability to restrict the flow of ideas and dialogue in this nation. If this argument is typical of the private sector, then the FCC has done the right thing by stepping in now to prevent ISPs from becoming the *de facto* censors of the Internet.

Ending Paid Prioritization Agreements versus Broadband Expansion. Net neutrality encompasses more than neutrally handling data and website access. It also requires an end to the paid prioritization agreements which have long been promoted as necessary to maintaining service quality for real-time applications like streaming video. Ending paid prioritization carries with it economic and engineering concerns other aspects of the Order lack. Nearly everyone can understand that neutral handling of content removes from the networks the authority to censor content. Much of the popular support for net neutrality centers on anti-censorship and the American ideals of free speech and free expression. But prioritization touches on concerns which are less ideal and more practical.

By banning paid prioritization, the FCC has forced the issue of building more robust, high-speed broadband infrastructure. To avoid degradation in service quality, networks must incur greater expenses to build increased bandwidth. The Connect America Fund subsidizes these costs for networks willing to meet minimum speed requirements (Brodkin, 2014). To support experiments to bring broadband to rural areas, the FCC plans to release $100 million from the Fund, which is supported by the Universal Service program (Engebretson, 2014). Recent awards include more than $16 million to four companies in November 2015, with the goal of bringing broadband to areas in five states, and the FCC has planned a reverse auction for other carriers to step in (Arnason, 2015). The FCC clearly wants to stimulate broadband expansion, refusing to incentivize lower-capacity networks that could allow companies to profit from prioritization payments without increasing their capacity. After all, a scarcity of capacity forces the demand for prioritization, and generates a profit without improving infrastructure.

Wireless has a role to play in this broadband expansion. In the AT&T wireless broadband initiative mentioned earlier, we see an example of a possible solution to the expensive infrastructure problems posed by a prohibition on blocking and throttling. Bandwidth is not infinite, and if broadband companies seek to maintain quality of service in real-time streaming applications, they will need infrastructure that can meet those demands without restricting less time-sensitive data flows. Wireless broadband initiatives, if successful, may shift the economic pressure away from installing expensive last-mile fixed-line cable services. Instead, they will create a push for freeing up spectrum frequencies, which has been the goal of recent FCC spectrum auctions. The advantages to such auctions, though beyond the scope of this essay, are compelling enough that since the FCC began the first of more than thirty such auctions in 1994, the U.S. model has been emulated by many nations around the world pursuing the same spectrum usage goals (Cramton, 2001, p.1).

Reasonable Network Management Practices. With these arguments about prioritization versus expansion in mind, one other aspect of the 2015 Order bears examining. Because infrastructure expansion does not happen overnight, networks have received some wiggle room in the language of "reasonable" network management practices to ensure quality of service. The 2015 Order makes allowances for practices required to effectively manage a network, but what are these practices, and what is reasonable? As we have seen, leaving things to a judgment call often means that a federal judge will have to field these questions.

On the one hand, this sounds like the persistence of the same vague language which has plagued the FCC's efforts and undermined its authority for years. One can easily imagine a new glut of lawsuits asking state and federal judges to determine whether or not a management practice is reasonable—a seemingly endless exercise in subjectivity. But on the other hand, a one-size-fits-all definition of reasonable practices is a poor alternative. What may be reasonable with today's technology may cease to be reasonable as technology evolves, and it is a failure to allow for rapidly changing technology which has caused much of the legal problems under the 1996 Act.

Though Commissioner Maureen K. Ohlhausen of the Federal Trade Commission objects to the 2015 Order, she makes a good argument for the importance of deciding some matters on a case-by-case basis. Describing the "history of the FCC" as "a series of regulatory attempts... to fit new technologies and business models into an increasingly out-of-date regulatory model", she points out that "statutory, procedural, and resource constraints make it impossible for the FCC" to keep up with the "trends of a very complex and rapidly evolving industry" (Ohlhausen, 2015, p. 209). She then contrasts this with the FTC's "enforcement-centric rather than rule-making-centric" approach which allows it to address "deceptive or unfair practices" on a "case-by-case" basis instead of attempting to make one-size-fits-all rules (ibid, p. 212). Ohlhausen criticizes the 2015 Order's Title II reclassification of broadband for potentially reducing "the FTC's authority to protect consumers online" because common carrier services "are outside of the FTC's jurisdiction" (ibid, p. 229). But on the other hand, her admonitions to reduce the silos created by separate Titles and to adopt a more flexible, case-by-case approach suggest that the 2015 Order's requirement for undefined reasonability in network management is the right track for the FCC. If the FCC has decided it will be the agency to handle these matters, then it is doing the right thing by leaving itself room for flexibility instead of trying to rigidly define network management in an ever-changing world.

VI. AFFIRMING THE FCC'S 2015 OPEN INTERNET ORDER.

A Clear and Current Standard of Authority. Given the difficult history of categorizing and regulating broadband Internet access, the FCC has made the right decision by bringing it under Title II authority. Technology has converged since the dawn of the Internet, but legal definitions and policies have failed to similarly converge. Federal regulation has lagged hopelessly behind technological advances which have reinvented and redefined the nature of telecommunications for the twenty-first century.

Regulating the various means of telecommunications based on the physical structures which originally carried them makes no sense in the digital age. All of the telecommunication services which originated on fixed-line, copper-wire, analog networks can now take place on digital networks, and so can all of the services formerly reliant on radio waves, as well as all services which began digitally. Regulation has treated differently the transmission of voice communication, audio entertainment, video conferencing, and Internet access as discretely different services based on a model of physical networks which no longer applies.

This increasingly nonsensical regulatory approach has plagued the courts long enough. It has wasted the time and resources of state and federal judges for decades, requiring them to interpret vague and poorly crafted laws. Judges have had to examine and re-examine the FCC's actions concerning highly technical matters more suited to engineers and economists, all in the context of outdated legislation which does not clearly apply to today's technology. The lack of legislative clarity about the FCC's proper scope of authority has resulted in expensive litigations that sap the energy of the FCC and the courts alike. The new Title II classification of broadband Internet access provides the agency a consistent and clear framework which, if not undermined by the courts and Congress, will greatly simplify the relevant legal questions and regulatory decisions.

Congress and the courts need to follow the FCC's lead in catching up with technological reality. This executive action gives a wake-up call to the legislative and judicial branches that times and technology have changed, and we cannot expect to efficiently regulate a new world using old and irrelevant approaches. Fortunately, judges at the state and federal level have expressed, even if only in dissenting opinions or in subsequently overruled decisions, a belief that broadband truly should be classified as a telecommunication service and not an information service. This bodes well for future judicial activity, as it shows many judges already favor this position, and have probably been wondering when the FCC would face facts.

Congress, on the other hand, subject to intense lobbying pressures from industry giants who have profited from the outdated classification regime, may be more reluctant to jump on the Title II bandwagon. It may be easier to get the nine justices of the Supreme Court to validate the 2015 Open Internet order than to build agreement amongst hundreds of legislators influenced by special interest groups.

Weathering the Legal Backlash. But even with the support of the other branches of government, the FCC's intended expansion of broadband Internet access will face obstacles. In Congress, the House Appropriations Committee recently confronted two amendments to the 2016 financial services and general government bill. As *Telecommunications Reports* explained, these amendments, which the Committee rejected, would have barred the FCC from implementing the 2015 Order until pending court cases had been resolved, prevented the FCC from using fiscal year 2016 funding "to directly or indirectly regulate charges or data usage limits for broadband Internet access" (including doing so through "enforcement actions"), and prohibited the FCC from enforcing any rule it had not published on its website "not later than 21 days before the date on which the vote occurs" (Kirby, 2015, p. 22). Clearly, congressional opponents of the 2015 Order were not above loading a general spending bill with ammunition against the FCC.

The FCC also had to deal with a number of requests to stay the Order, requests made by corporations in the Internet industry such as U.S. Telecom Association, AT&T, and CenturyLink; American Cable Association and the National Cable Association; and Daniel Berninger of the Voice Communications Exchange Committee (FCC Denies Requests, 2015, p. 15). The FCC denied them on the basis that "no irreparable harm" to the broadband companies had been shown. The parties to these denied requests then turned them into lawsuits for the Circuit Court to wade through. Ignoring the *Brand X* decision that the classification of broadband was the FCC's to decide, these companies argued that "broadband Internet access 'fits squarely' within the statutory definition of Communication Act Title I information services" (ibid). One of these cases is the US Telecom Association case covered in the previous section on "free speech" arguments.

On top of that, states have begun to challenge the FCC's decision, reached on the same day as the vote on the 2015 Order, to preempt state laws that have prevented municipalities from building their own broadband networks. On the forefront of this litigation stand Tennessee and North Carolina, each of which has limits on publicly created Internet service (Fung, 2015). In other areas, like the city of Chanute, Kansas, municipalities are taking it upon themselves to fill a service void left by broadband corporations (Lefler, 2014). While this approach fits in with Chairman Wheeler's vision of expanding broadband access, "nineteen states have such laws, often passed at the behest of private Internet service providers that didn't want to face competition" (Brodkin, 2015). The FCC may have achieved a more solid legal framework for its authority by reclassifying broadband, but its judicial battles are not yet over.

Leveling the Playing Field of Prioritization. The FCC has taken the right action to support worthy long-term goals, but the massive complexity of the infrastructure and political realities means neither a smooth nor unobstructed path in the short term. In particular, doing away with paid prioritization challenges the status quo so deeply that it will produce both engineering and economic downsides. Despite these challenges, it is worth considering the flip side of the coin. Everyone wants their data transmitted at the best and fastest possible speed. No one wants to be left behind. Therefore, everyone has an interest in being prioritized. If we assume that everyone with such a desire can eventually muster the funds to pay for prioritization, then the logical result is the prioritization of everything.

In such a scenario, no one wins anything. The playing field would once again become level. Everyone paying for priority results in the same equality as no one paying for it; i.e., everyone gets the same treatment. Therefore, although paid prioritization makes sense at the outset when not everyone has paid for it yet, it wastes resources in a race that ultimately leads nowhere. The FCC's contentious ban on paid prioritization makes more sense in this light. The ban merely prevents this nonsensical and utterly doomed race to nowhere, and instead forces attention on how we can build more robust networks in an atmosphere of equal treatment and innovation.

VII. CONCLUSION.

Those who value the Internet for free and open access to data, information, and connection to others at reasonable prices will agree with the FCC's recent decision to bring broadband Internet under the umbrella of telecommunication services. By treating broadband access as a common carriage service, the FCC is in a greater position to prevent networks from censoring and limiting citizens' access to data—data we need to learn about and understand our increasingly complex world, and must increasingly rely on for our professional and economic well-being. Reclassifying broadband under Title II effectively solves a longstanding problem for the agency and federal courts.

ANNOTATED BIBLIOGRAPHY

Alexis [knothing]. (26 February 2015). "Thank you, reddit. Your efforts led to an historic FCC ruling and this note from the President of the United States." *Blog.Reddit*. http://www.redditblog.com/2015/02/thank-you-reddit-your-efforts-led-to.html

An example of online grass-roots political activism regarding net neutrality, and the high volume of response the FCC received as a result.

Arnason, Bernie. (16 November 2015). "FCC Releases $16 Million for Rural Broadband Experiments Funding." *Telecompetitor*. http://www.telecompetitor.com/fcc-releases-16-million-for-rural-broadband-experiments-funding/

Brief for Respondents. (14 September 2015). USCA Case #15-1063, *United States Telecom Association v. FCC*. Document #1573000. https://assets.documentcloud.org/documents/2423172/oifinalasfiled.pdf

FCC responds to, among other things, the accusations of censorship and violations of First Amendment.

Brodkin, Jon. (17 September 2014). "Sorry, AT&T and Verizon: 4Mbps isn't fast enough for 'broadband': FCC chairman says Americans shouldn't subsidize Internet service under 10Mbps." *ArsTechnica*. http://arstechnica.com/business/2014/09/sorry-att-and-verizon-4mbps-isnt-fast-enough-for-broadband/

This article summarizes Chairman Wheeler's remarks before a House committee regarding a minimal acceptable speed for broadband Internet access, and its relation to subsidies from the Connect America Fund.

Brodkin, Jon. (26 February 2015). "FCC overturns state laws that protect ISPs from local competition: Municipal broadband networks could expand because of FCC's controversial vote." *ArsTechnica.*
http://arstechnica.com/business/2015/02/fcc-overturns-state-laws-that-protect-isps-from-local-competition/

Cramton, Peter. (February 2001). Spectrum Auctions. In (2002) Cave, Martin, et. al., (Eds.), *Handbook of Telecommunications Economics, Vol. 1: Structure, Regulation, and Competition*, Chapter 14, pp. 605-639. Oxford, UK: Elsevier.
http://www.cramton.umd.edu/papers2000-2004/01hte-spectrum-auctions.pdf

Cramton's chapter gives a history of spectrum auctions and their advantages to the public, corporations, and governments.

"Court Plans Speedy Review of Open Internet Order." (1 July 2015). *Telecommunications Reports, 81*(13), 5-7.

Paragraphs 4-5: The DC Circuit Court in 2014 "overturned blocking and non-discrimination rules adopted in a 2010 FCC order as the impermissible application of de facto common carrier regulation to services that were not at the time classified as common carrier services" (p. 5). US Telecom Association and "other parties" requested the US Court of Appeals for the District of Columbia stay the 2015 reclassification of broadband as telecom, a stay which would therefore render the anti-blocking provisions unenforceable (p. 5).

The Court rejected this request but granted expedition in hearing *US Telecom Association v FCC* (case 15-1063) and similar cases to be consolidated. Page 7, paragraph 1 offers an argument that banning editorial discretion of ISPs equates to government censorship.

Engebretson, Joan. (12 November 2014). "FCC: Rural Broadband Experiment Funding to Be Awarded in 'Coming Weeks'." *Telecompetitor*. http://www.telecompetitor.com/fcc-rural-broadband-experiment-funding-awarded-coming-weeks/

"FCC Denies Requests to Stay Open Internet Order for Not Citing 'Concrete' Harms; Eyes Turn to Court." (15 May 2015). *Telecommunications Reports*, 81(10), 15-16.

Some stay requests mentioned in "Court Plans Speedy Review of Open Internet Order" were originally stay requests to the FCC by the companies who later filed with the DC Circuit: US Telecom Association, AT&T, and CenturyLink; American Cable Association and the National Cable Association; and Daniel Berninger of the Voice Communications Exchange Committee.

The article clarifies aspects of Title II regulation historically applied to telephone companies but which are not being applied to broadband access under the new Order, "including rate regulations, tariffing, last-mile unbundling, and obligations to contribute to the Universal Service Fund" (p. 15, column 1, last paragraph).

Joint petitioners in subsequent stay requests to the Circuit Court object, in part, to the reclassification "because broadband Internet access 'fits squarely' within the statutory definition of Communication Act

Title I information services" (p. 15, column 2, third paragraph column 2). Article quotes the FCC's brief which denies "irreparable harm" to the broadband companies.

Federal Communications Commission. (4 February 2015). *Chairman Wheeler Proposes New Rules for Protecting the Open Internet.* https://www.fcc.gov/document/chairman-wheeler-proposes-new-rules-protecting-open-internet

Statement of proposal to reclassify broadband access under Title II.

Federal Communications Commission. (adopted 26 February 2015; released 12 March 2015). *FCC-15-24A1: Report and Order on Remand, Declaration Ruling, and Order* (Commonly called the 2015 Open Internet Order). https://apps.fcc.gov/edocs_public/attachmatch/FCC-15-24A1.pdf

Full text of the 2015 Open Internet Order.

Federal Communications Commission. (February 2015). *Statement of Chairman Tom Wheeler RE: Protecting and Promoting the Open Internet, GN Docket No. 14-28.* https://apps.fcc.gov/edocs_public/attachmatch/DOC-332260A2.pdf

Wheeler's statement briefly explains the new Title II classification of broadband, and summarizes the main "bright-line" rules of the 2015 Order.
See also the FCC's summary of the 2015 Order: (26 February 2015). *FCC Adopts Strong, Sustainable Rules to Protect the Open Internet.*

https://www.fcc.gov/document/fcc-adopts-strong-sustainable-rules-protect-open-internet

See also the FCC Open Internet Webpage at https://www.fcc.gov/openinternet

"Bright-line" rules summarized as:

No Blocking: broadband providers may not block access to legal content, applications, services, or non-harmful devices.

No Throttling: broadband providers may not impair or degrade lawful Internet traffic on the basis of content, applications, services, or non-harmful devices.

No Paid Prioritization: broadband providers may not favor some lawful Internet traffic over other lawful traffic in exchange for consideration of any kind—in other words, no "fast lanes." This rule also bans ISPs from prioritizing content and services of their affiliates.

Fung, Brian. (15 September 2014). "The FCC has now received 3 million net neutrality comments." *The Washington Post.*
https://www.washingtonpost.com/news/the-switch/wp/2014/09/15/the-fcc-has-now-received-3-million-net-neutrality-comments/

Fung, Brian. (9 November 2015). Obama championed cheap, fast, city-run Internet. His administration won't." *The Washington Post.*
https://www.washingtonpost.com/news/the-switch/wp/2015/11/09/the-fccs-intervention-on-city-run-broadband-may-be-in-trouble/

Jacobs, Rebecca, and Palchick, Mark. (4 May 2015). "Highlights of the 2015 Open Internet Order." *Wombe Carlye* (Client Report).
http://www.wcsr.com/resources/pdfs/telecomm050414.pdf

Executive summary of the main points of the 2015 Order, including what the Order does not apply to (such as premises operators, dial-up, etc.). This report clarifies that broadband will be subject to sections 201, 202, and 208 of the Communications Act; privacy requirements of Section 222; and the disability provisions of 225, 251(a)(2), and 255. It explains that ISPs are required to comply with Section 254 (provides for promoting universal broadband) but not to contribute to the Universal Service Fund. Includes a table showing what Sections "forbearance" applies to.

Joint Brief for Petitioners Alamo Broadband Inc. and Daniel Berninger. (30 July 2015). USCA Case #15-1063, *United States Telecom Association v. FCC*. Document #1565433. https://assets.documentcloud.org/documents/2423210/alamo-net-neutrality-brief.pdf

Full text of the Joint Brief. The petitioners argue, among other things, that the FCC's new rules prohibiting them from effectively censoring by blocking content actually equate to censorship in violation of the First Amendment.

Kirby, Paul. (1 July 2015). "House Appropriations Committee Retains Open Internet Order Stay." *Telecommunications Reports*, *81*(13), 22-24.

Explains some Congressional response to the 2015 Order; namely, the addition (and subsequent rejection) of anti-FCC amendments to a spending bill.

Lefler, Dion. (24 May 2014). "Chanute aims to provide speedy Internet service to all homes, businesses in

town." *Wichita Eagle.*
http://www.kansas.com/news/article1144149.html

Levy, Josh. (24 April 2014). "We are fighting to restore Net Neutrality. Ask us anything. (Josh Levy from Free Press, David Segal from Demand Progress, Amalia Deloney of Center for Media Justice, First Amendment lawyer Marvin Ammori & Sarah Morris of Open Technology Institute)." *Reddit.* Archived post https://www.reddit.com/r/IAmA/comments/23vddm/ we_are_fighting_to_restore_net_neutrality_ask_us

Nagesh, Gautham. (7 May 2014). Amazon, Google, Facebook and Others Disagree With FCC Rules on Net Neutrality: Firms, Commissioners Voice Concerns With New Rules That Threaten 'Net Neutrality'." *The Wall Street Journal.*
http://www.wsj.com/news/articles/SB100014240527023 0370130457954836415420512б

Nuechterlein, Jonathan E., and Weiser, Philip J. (2013). *Digital Crossroads: Telecommunications Law and Policy in the Internet Age. 2nd Edition.* Cambridge, MA: MIT Press.

College textbook with an excellent background on the technology of the Internet, along with the political and legal environment of regulating it. Although it examines the history of the net neutrality movement, the book admits that at the time of publication, much remained to be settled in the courts and at the FCC. The issuance of the 2015 Order settled many of the questions posed in the text.

Ohlhausen, Maureen K. (April 2015). "The FCC's Knowledge Problem: How to Protect Consumers

Online." *Federal Communications Law Journal*, 67(2), 204-234. http://www.fclj.org/wp-content/uploads/2015/09/67.2.2_Ohlhausen.pdf

In 2006, author was Director of the Federal Trade Commission's Office of Policy Planning, leading the FTC's inquiry into net neutrality, which produced the 2007 report "Broadband Connectivity Competition Policy". Pages 208-212 summarize the problems of trying to regulate the modern telecom/internet environment, which is perpetually changing, with one-size-fits-all rules that cannot help but lag behind industry realities.

Chapter 2 addresses net neutrality and the FCC. 2A sums up the major arguments for and against net neutrality. 2B reviews the history of classifying always-on cable Internet access as an information service under Title I; the Verizon decision striking down the anti-blocking aspects of the 2010 Open Internet Order; and the development of the 2015 Order. Chapter 3A critiques specific provisions of the 2015 Order, pointing out that paid prioritization has benefits.

Author argues that reclassifying broadband under Title II (common carrier) removes it from FTC jurisdiction, although the FTC leads the world in privacy and data security enforcement, and has protected consumers many times from deceptive or unfair behaviors of broadband providers.

Reed, Brad. (1 October 2015). "AT&T Is Testing New Tech That Delivers Home Broadband Service Wirelessly." *BGR (Boy Genius Report)*. http://bgr.com/2015/10/01/att-fixed-wireless-broadband-test/

Ruane, Kathleen Ann. (26 March 2014). *Net Neutrality: The FCC's Authority to Regulate Broadband Internet Traffic*

Management. (CRS Report R40234). Congressional
Research Service.
https://www.fas.org/sgp/crs/misc/R40234.pdf

Author is a legislative attorney. The report was prepared
for members and committees of Congress and
published a year before the 2015 Order. It examines the
2010 Order and the subsequent *Verizon v FCC* case. The
DC Circuit Court in *Verizon* found that the 2010 Order's
anti-discrimination and anti-blocking provisions
exceeded the FCC's Title I authority over "information
services", which was the FCC's current classification of
broadband. See page 4, paragraph 1 for an analysis of
Brand X where the Supreme Court decided the FCC
could classify broadband.

The report gives a succinct history of the
classification of broadband and its relation to the
Telecommunications Act (Section 706, specifically),
Title I ("ancillary" authority), and Title II (common
carrier). See pages 9-10 for a highlight of relevant
passages from Section 706. See page 12 for a summary of
what "common carrier" means.

Ruiz, Rebecca R., and Lohr, Steve. (26 February 2015).
"FCC Approves Net Neutrality Rules, Classifying
Broadband Internet Service as a Utility". *The New York
Times*.
http://www.nytimes.com/2015/02/27/technology/net-
neutrality-fcc-vote-internet-utility.html?_r=0

Signaigo, Amy L. (Spring, 2007). National Cable &
Telecommunications Association v. Brand X Internet
Services: Resolving Irregularities in Regulation?
*Northwestern Journal of Technology and Intellectual
Property*, 5(2): Article 8 (PDF not paginated).

http://scholarlycommons.law.northwestern.edu/cgi/vi
ewcontent.cgi?article=1147&context=njtip

Author was a JD candidate at Northwestern University
School of Law, with a background in hardware
engineering and a Bachelor's in Computer and Electrical
Engineering from Purdue. The article examines *Brand X*.
It explains why the Ninth Circuit Court applied the
Portland decision rather than *Chevron*; *Portland* being
its own ruling that broadband was a telecom service not
an information service.
    Section IV examines the difficulties of this case,
especially how they stem from the classifications of
telecommunications versus information services, and it
argues the classifications need changed or eliminated.
Section V offers a critique of inconsistencies within FCC
broadband policy.

Singleton, Micah. (29 January 2015). "The FCC has changed
    the definition of broadband: The minimum broadband
    download speeds now begin at 25Mbps, up from
    4Mbps." *The Verge*.
    http://www.theverge.com/2015/1/29/7932653/fcc-
    changed-definition-broadband-25mbps

Stanley, Jay. (October 2010). Network Neutrality 101: *Why
    the Government Must Act to Preserve the Free and Open
    Internet*. American Civil Liberties Union (ACLU).
    https://www.aclu.org/files/assets/ACLU_report_-
    _Network_Neutrality_101_October_2010.pdf

Tatel, David S. (14 January 2014). United States Court of
    Appeals for the District of Columbia Circuit. *Verizon v.
    Federal Communications Commission*, 740 F.3d 623, 11-
    1355.
    https://www.cadc.uscourts.gov/internet/opinions.nsf/3

af8b4d938cdeea685257c6000532062/$file/11-1355-
1474943.pdf

Thomas, Clarence. (27 June 2005). United States Supreme
Court. *National Cable & Telecommunications Ass'n v.
Brand X Internet Services*, 545 U.S. 967. (Justice
Thomas for the majority, Justice Scalia dissenting.)
http://www.techlawjournal.com/courts2003/brandx/br
andx_scus.pdf

United States Congress. (3 January 1996).
Telecommunications Act of 1996.
http://transition.fcc.gov/Reports/tcom1996.pdf

White House, Office of the Press Secretary. (9 May 2013).
"Presidential Nominations Sent to the Senate."
WhiteHouse.Gov. https://www.whitehouse.gov/the-
press-office/2013/05/09/presidential-nominations-
sent-senate-0

I. BACKGROUND AND SUMMARY OF CASE.

In February 2015, the FCC released the 2015 Open Internet Order. Among other things, the Order reclassified broadband Internet access as a telecommunications service subject to common carrier regulation under the FCC's Title II authority, pursuant to authority granted by the Telecommunications Act of 1996. Litigation in federal courts has already begun to challenge the FCC's new regulatory scheme, including the FCC's authority to change broadband's existing classification from an information service regulated under Title I (in which it was not subject to common carrier regulatory practices).

However, *Brand X* clarifies the Supreme Court's perception of this authority. Although in *Brand X* the Court upheld the FCC's authority to classify broadband as an information service and not a telecommunications service, the rationale of the majority opinion clearly supports the opposite decision, too. *Brand X* recognizes the FCC's authority to make this decision, regardless of which way it decides to classify.

The opinion discussed in this case study was issued concurrently on June 17, 2005 with the certiorari on *Federal Communications Commission et al v. Brand X Internet Services et al*. It reverses the decision of the Ninth Circuit Court of Appeals which had ruled against the FCC's classification of broadband as an information service. The Ninth Circuit had reasoned that because cable modems used telecommunications technology, classifying broadband as telecommunication service was the *best* interpretation of The Telecommunications Act of 1996. The Ninth Circuit reasoned that since the FCC did not make the best interpretation, the agency's classification could be struck down by the court. Supreme Court Justice Thomas' majority opinion found fault with the Ninth Circuit's reasoning.

II. MAJOR POINTS OF REASONING.

The majority found the FCC's construction of language from the Telecommunications Act of 1996 to be well within its lawful authority. Much of the opinion provides a primer on internet technology, both emerging and converging at that time. It gives the appropriate technological and policy background for why the thorny distinctions between "information" and "telecommunication" services exist in the first place. Given the complexity of this discussion, it suffices to say it allowed the Court to assert that the FCC's interpretation of The Act was, in fact, reasonable. That it may not have been the *best* or even the *only* interpretation was beside the point to the Court, so long as it was *reasonable*.

In terms of precedent, the Court disapproved of the Ninth Circuit's use of *AT&T Corp. v. Portland* which held that cable modem was a telecommunications service. The Court asserted that the proper precedent to use was *Chevron*. The Court's reasoning began first with establishing the ambiguity of The Act, an ambiguity immediately obvious upon *any* reading of the legislation, and a persistent regulatory problem in more cases than this one.

The Court then uses this ambiguity to establish *Chevron* as the correct precedent in such a case: "If a statute is ambiguous, and if the implementing agency's construction is reasonable, *Chevron* requires a federal court to accept the agency's construction of the statute, even if the agency's reading differs from what the court believes is the best statutory interpretation. *Id.*, at 843-844, and n. 11" (Thomas, 2005, p. 8).

Therefore, the majority opinion in *Brand X* clearly established:

1. The Telecommunications Act of 1996 is ambiguous regarding the definitions and classifications of "telecommunications services" versus "information services", and

2. This ambiguity affords the FCC the authority to classify the services and create regulation based on a reasonable interpretation of the given wording, and

3. This interpretation does *not* need to agree with any particular court's preferred reading of the ambiguity but must only be reasonable, and

4. In such a scenario where a court might read The Act differently than the FCC might, the courts must defer to the FCC (per *Chevron*).

In short, the FCC has authority under the ambiguous terms of the Telecommunications Act of 1996 to classify cable modem internet access as either information service (regulated under Title I) *or* telecommunications service (regulated under Title II) as it sees fit. Therefore, when considering the 2015 Open Internet Order, it is entirely reasonable to accept the FCC's authority to now reclassify broadband as a telecommunications service (Title II) despite its earlier classification to the contrary, for this classification power rightly belongs to the FCC.

III. Dissenting Opinion.

Justice Scalia's dissenting opinion focuses on his belief that because a cable modem has a telecommunications function, it by definition renders broadband cable Internet access a telecommunications service. This contrasts with majority arguments that the essential service provided as broadband Internet access is, by definition, an information service, and the modem is simply a functionally inseparable tool for providing the actual underlying service.

Scalia's dissent also argued that the "*Chevron* deference" to agency interpretation gave federal agencies a dangerous amount of power to take "action that the Supreme Court found unlawful" by creating an environment where "judicial decisions" are "subject to reversal by Executive officers" (p. 14, p. 13).

IV. CONCLUSION.

If the distinction between "information" and "telecommunication" services appears confusing and arbitrary, it is exactly this artificial and legally cumbersome distinction between converging technologies the 2015 Open Internet Order seeks to eliminate. While the majority may have been correct on their legal definitions, Scalia too was correct in his insight that these technologies could not logically or meaningfully be separated.

The FCC's interpretation of its authority pursuant to *Brand X* agrees with this analysis. Section C.43 of the 2015 Order refers to both the majority and dissenting opinions of this case.

REFERENCES

Federal Communications Commission. (adopted 26 February 2015; released 12 March 2015). *FCC-15-24A1: Report and Order on Remand, Declaration Ruling, and Order* (Commonly called the 2015 Open Internet Order). https://apps.fcc.gov/edocs_public/attachmatch/FCC-15-24A1.pdf

Panner, Owen M. (3 June 1999). *AT&T Corp. v. City of Portland*, 43 F. Supp. 2d 1146 (D. Or. 1999). https://www.courtlistener.com/opinion/2423001/at-t-corp-v-city-of-portland/

Stevens, John Paul. (25 June 1984). United States Supreme Court. *Chevron USA Inc. v Natural Resources Defense Council, Inc.*, 467 U.S. 837. https://www.law.cornell.edu/supremecourt/text/467/837

Thomas, Clarence. (27 June 2005). United States Supreme Court. *National Cable & Telecommunications Ass'n v. Brand X Internet Services*, 545 U.S. 967. (Justice Thomas writing for the majority, Justice Scalia dissenting.) http://www.techlawjournal.com/courts2003/brandx/brandx_scus.pdf

Two Years of Net Neutrality: A Policy Analysis Follow-Up

I. Introduction: Happy Anniversary

In December 2015, I covered the history and meaning of the **FCC's 2015 Open Internet Order**. February 26, 2017 is the nation's two-year anniversary with this policy, and it arrives at time where a shift in federal power heralds a new era and a potentially new policy direction.

In my previous analysis, I examined the arguments made by Alamo Broadband and others in documents presented to the court in on-going proceedings in *USTA v. FCC*. Since then, the Court of Appeals issued its decision in 2016. The court settled the matter in agreement with the FCC's position on the Order. This decision is unlikely to be reviewed by the Supreme Court, so I will summarize its implications in Part I.

The FCC exercised its newfound Title II authority to issue three enforcement orders related to privacy and security, generally in the form of monetary fines and procedural requirements. Though most everyone agrees on the importance of data security and privacy, the net neutrality aspects of the Order continue to draw criticism. Critics argue that net neutrality stifles innovation, and they present less neutral policies in other nations as a critique of the Order. But the most pointed criticism of the Order, and of the *USTA* decision, came from within the FCC itself—from former Commissioner Pai, now appointed FCC Chairman by President Trump in the wake of Tom Wheeler's resignation.

This power shift, given the FCC's tendency toward strongly partisan votes, could threaten Wheeler's vision of broadband expansion at higher speeds into all areas of the nation. Wheeler spoke in favor of municipal broadband, challenging the recent court decisions on the matter.

Exploring these developments in the legal, administrative, and political dimensions of the Order's first two years will shed light on the future of the Order, current critiques of net neutrality, and the Order's current relation to the more general policy goal of broadband expansion.

II. *USTA v. FCC:* THE RESOLUTION.

USTA v. FCC (2016) was not decided until more than a year into the new Title II policy regime. The arguments presented by the corporate plaintiffs were covered in detail in my first analysis, and I predicted the Court of Appeals for the District of Columbia Circuit would decide for itself what the Supreme Court had already solved in *Brand X*; namely, that the FCC had the authority to classify broadband under Title II and was reasonably interpreting the language of its guiding legislation.

1. A Not-So-New Decision. The heart of *USTA v. FCC* was an objection to the FCC's ban on paid prioritization. Arguments from co-plaintiff Alamo Broadband appealed to a First Amendment interpretation of the broadband provider's role. Determining not to provide access to Internet content the ISP finds objectionable would, in this view, constitute an exercise of the ISP's free speech. The court found no merit in free speech arguments (Fung, 2016). And understandably so. Censoring content is the opposite of free speech.

An analysis in *Houston Law Review* argued in favor of a split interpretation of First Amendment protection. As neutral transmitters of data, ISPs are not really speaking. But Stephanie Kan proposes that when ISPs function as "edge providers", then courts should consider them as having free speech rights within the boundaries of the content *they create* and exercise *editorial control* over (Kan, 2016). Kan's "split" interpretation of free speech in ISP cases shows sensitivity to the significant difference in two functions: one, providing access to all content; two, content creation.

It was not free speech but a more procedural matter that decided *USTA*: the FCC's authority to classify broadband under Title II. *Brand X* had established the Supreme Court's view of this question, and the Court of Appeals reaffirmed it with similar reasoning. This court used the reasoning from *Chevron*, but the legal questions asked were the same: is the 1996 Act vague about how broadband should be classified, and does the FCC have the authority to make a definite classification? Yes, and yes.

This decision should end the questioning of the FCC's authority to classify broadband. The agency has successfully established an interpretation of its defining congressional statute which the judiciary will agree with. Given that lengthy, costly litigation has for too long drawn agency resources away from its true policy goals, this solid scheme of regulatory authority will simplify things. This is why "the FCC opted for a reclassification that offered a stronger legal foundation for its regulatory authority" (WSGR, 2015).

USTA answers the question of whether or not this regulatory regime includes wireless broadband. "These two changes—reclassification under Title II and the regulation of mobile broadband—are the main focus of industry's legal challenge and were the subject of significant questioning at the recent hearing in the court of appeals" (ibid). The court determined Title II classification applied to wireless, and it found no reason to object to the FCC's inclusion of both wireless and wired service (Fung, 2016). Though the FCC had at one time "excluded mobile services from many of its net neutrality rules" in the early days of that marketplace, recent technological advances and "widespread use" prompted the FCC to apply its regulations to both fixed and mobile broadband (WSGR, 2015).

Chairman Wheeler acknowledged the "decade of debate and legal battles" leading up to this affirmation of the FCC's authority. But not everyone felt the matter was completely settled.

2. Will the Fight Go On? Because this was an opinion issued by a three-judge panel, not all the court's judges, the plaintiffs could request all the judges hear the case, or possibly ask for a review from the Supreme Court (Brodkin, 2016). AT&T general counsel claimed to have "always expected this issue to be decided by the Supreme Court" (Qtd. in Kang, 14 Jun. 2016). But it sounds like so much saber-rattling. Why would the Supreme Court waste its time hearing this case when it already stated its position in *Brand X*?

The durability of this decision does not come without its dissenters and detractors at the court, at the ISPs, and within the FCC. Dissenting judge Stephen Williams voiced concern about discouraging competition in the broadband industry (ibid). The National Cable and Telecommunications Association called upon Congress to settle the matter by drafting new legislation (ibid). The NCTA may be right; better legislation would have prevented much litigation, but that is exactly the long-standing problem the new regulatory scheme evolved from and has now solved.

Commissioner Ajit Pai, now Chairman, opposed the Title II regime to begin with. In the wake of *USTA*, he voiced his support for the plaintiffs, saying, "these regulations are unlawful, and I hope that the parties challenging them will continue the legal fight" (Qtd. in ibid). What's more likely is that federal courts have sufficient agreement about the FCC's scope of authority, and the 2016 decision will serve as precedent for other courts. But even if the matter is iron-clad on the judicial front, Chairman Pai's ongoing and open objections to the Title II regime could undo these two years of support from the judiciary.

III. Enforcing Privacy and Security Under Title II.

Not all the developments in the FCC's new regulatory scheme had to do with paid prioritization or clarifying that broadband means *all* broadband, wired or not. The FCC also used its Title II authority to enforce matters of security and privacy, which often get less media attention. These enforcement actions garner less dissent than net neutrality, possibly because no matter where you stand on net neutrality, you probably want your private data secure. It's something everyone can agree on, and examining this aspect of Title II enforcement puts the Order in a less controversial light.

1. **TerraCom & YourTel.** A $3.5M action against TerraCom & YourTel was the "agency's first data security action against a telecom provider" (WSGR, 2015). The enforcement order identifies the violation clearly: "The Companies' vendor stored the proprietary information of more than 300,000 customers in clear, readable text on servers that were accessible over the Internet, and the data was not password protected or encrypted" (FCC, Order DA 15-776).

The FCC did more than fine these companies. It defined administrative procedures the companies needed to implement, from "designating a senior corporate manager who is a certified privacy professional" to filing regular compliance reports with the FCC (ibid). The FCC clearly sees in such a deplorable lack of data security a sign that these companies need to be told how to run a secure operation, and that they will be monitored until they get it right.

2. Cox Communications. After TerraCom, the FCC "brought its first privacy and data security enforcement action against a cable provider" (WSGR, 2015). Cox Communications entered a "seven-year consent decree" and agreed to "pay $595,000 to settle a case involving a hack that exposed the data of 61 Cox customers (almost $10,000 per customer)" (ibid).

What led to this security breach? According to the enforcement order, someone convinced a Cox customer service representative and a Cox contractor to enter their respective account IDs and passwords into a fake website, which the third party controlled. With those IDs and passwords, the third party could then access customer information within Cox's data systems (FCC, Order DA 15-1241). The enforcement order explains this is a common form of "social engineering", and that much of the customer information was then exposed through various social media sites. As with the Terracom action, Cox received some pointed advice on how to run a secure operation.

3. Verizon. The FCC hit Verizon with a fine, requirements to notify customers before gathering any of their data, and instructions to get permission "before sharing consumer data with third party partner" (Kang, 7 Mar. 2016). Verizon had been using "supercookies" to gather customer information to be used for targeted advertising. "Even among customers who had tried to delete regular cookies from their mobile browsers, the supercookies, or hidden code unique to each customer, were undeletable and used as a workaround to continue data collection" such as "a mobile subscriber's browsing history" which "third-party companies used ...to target ads to users" (ibid). The privacy violation was revealed by a Stanford Law School privacy scholar who was subsequently hired by the FCC as a chief technologist (Singer, 2015).

Announcements of this enforcement came at a time when the FCC was proposing new privacy rules, which were approved in October 2016. "The agency made privacy rules for phones and cable television in the past, but high-speed Internet providers, including AT&T and Verizon Communications, were not held to any privacy restrictions" (Kang, 27 Oct. 2016). Welcome to the world of Title II. It should be noted that jurisdictionally, the FCC ends and the FTC begins at web-based companies. The FCC can regulate telcos and broadband ISPs, but the Federal Trade Commission establishes consumer protection rules for web-based companies (ibid).

The new privacy rules were approved 3-2, which demonstrates how much one vote either way can determine FCC policy. Without Chairman Wheeler, an outspoken proponent of these privacy rules, how different would the FCC's policies have been these past two years? The answer is *radically* different, and the recent shift in political power could undermine much of what net neutrality advocates consider advances in protecting and expanding broadband Internet.

IV. INNOVATIVE OR NOT?
CRITIQUES OF THE ORDER.

1. **Priority Versus Speed.** A 2016 *TechPolicyDaily* column pointed out that despite the ban on paid prioritization, different connection speeds form *de facto* prioritization of data delivery to different customers using different speeds. Bronwyn Howell argued that a truly neutral net would deliver all information at the same speed, and not differentiate speeds between different customers. One Internet, one connection speed. While it is difficult to imagine how an infrastructure currently being constructed and expanded from older underlying infrastructure could ever achieve Howell's utopian conception, his arguments

suggest how we could conceive of a truly neutral net in terms of connection speed and data delivery.

Setting aside current pricing tiers for speeds to residential and commercial customers, variances in connection speeds often affect rural and underserved municipalities. Achieving a neutral net in terms of neutral speed means the bar must be raised at a national level. Hundreds of municipal broadband projects are bringing robust high-speed broadband to their communities by building their own systems, and their ability to do so is a major part of creating a net that is at once neutral and high-performing.

2. Priority, Price, and Packages. Critiques of the net neutrality aspect of the Order point to examples such as MetroPCS who, in 2011, attempted to offer a low-cost plan to wireless subscribers. The package included unlimited web browsing, but "free access to YouTube, courtesy of an arrangement with Google whereby the search giant helped optimize YouTube content for MetroPCS's capacity-constrained networks" (Watts, 2015, p.. 455). But this preferential treatment to YouTube appeared to FCC regulators to violate the concept of net neutrality (non-preferential treatment of content providers). MetroPCS had financial troubles and was eventually absorbed into T-Mobile.

Using MetroPCS as a case study for the "chilling effect" of net neutrality may be misguided. The provider's financial troubles existed before the new neutrality discussion of the YouTube deal, and the episode took place four years before the 2015 Open Internet Order. The FCC never took enforcement action against MetroPCS on this matter, having only looked into it at the request of certain corporations. MetroPCS has little to do with the first two years of regulatory practice under the Order.

However, a bit of furor tends to erupt over FCC "policy" even when no action or official order happens. The FCC occasionally issues a report about something it has looked into, and what the implications of a company's actions *may* be under current Title II thinking. Often, an outcry against the FCC's current policy is only a response to a line of thought proposed in a general report, not an actual enforcement action.

In a 2017 op-ed piece for The Hill, former deputy U.S. coordinator for international communications and information policy Scott Cleland criticized an FCC report—not an official action or enforcement, just a report—for being anti-customer and using net neutrality to stifle innovation (Cleland, 2017). The report pointed out that AT&T might have a neutrality violation if it gave its subsidiary DirecTV preferential treatment in a zero-rating plan. The report commented that if DirecTV were zero-rated at nominal cost, it would be preferential treatment if other services incurred a significant per-gigabyte cost (Coldewey, 2017). No action was taken or recommended in this report.

The complexities of *common-carrier regulation* are always more dry than emotionally loaded words such as *net neutrality*, which work better as a soundbite than an objective policy description. But Cleland's critique makes a valid point: regulation in the Order's first two years has curtailed, in the U.S., several approaches to pricing and service which are flourishing internationally.

One is the "social media plan", which bundles low-cost broadband with access to a limited number of popular social media sites. The idea is to give Internet access to the sites most commonly used, and make that cost-effective by not providing the entire Internet someone may not want or need on their phone. Similar plans give a preferential treatment to a single online email provider (Lyons, p. 468). "Feature phone access plans" such as Facebook Zero and Google Free Zone offer packages with stripped-down versions of the site features (such as text-only interfaces) that require less data capacity and can be used at no extra charge (ibid, p. 470-2). For those who want to only use a specific service, such as Skype, wireless providers are offering packages with fewer app services and lower costs.

At the heart of the arguments over whether or not such packages can be offered under current Title II regulations are questions of innovation and competition. Is a phone giving preferential access to Facebook or Google services helping or hindering the market and the economy? Supporters of these plans point to their increased use across the globe, and numbers showing they have helped more people in low-income or underserved areas get connected. Detractors point out it's a biased connection to a limited selection of the Internet's possibilities, and that the ubiquity of any given social media company on a huge network of phones could give it an overpowering edge on other companies looking to break into the market.

I believe innovation means more than bundling services into packages, and sometimes the difference between innovative pricing plans gets confused with innovation in actual products and technology. Critics who champion innovation need to show more than a clever price plan based on free social media apps, because they have little to say about the Order's relation to real technological innovations that will get full broadband Internet access to everyone.

3. Presidential Influence. The *Michigan Law Review* published work which criticizes the amount of influence the President has on the FCC, and the 2015 Open Internet Order is a case study for that critique. Democratic President Obama appointed Tom Wheeler, and openly advocated for the Order, encouraging the public to voice support for it (Watts, 2016, p. 717-8). Chairman Pai, who did not vote in favor of the order, declared the FCC had expanded its Title II Authority to include broadband "for one reason and one reason alone. President Obama told us to" (Qtd. in Watts,

p. 719). Will Chairman Pai be as susceptible to the influence of the Republican President who appointed him as Wheeler's successor?

Presidential appointments, and the Senate's confirmation process, do allow the executive and the legislature to influence policy by maintaining a party majority among the chairman and commissioners, especially given the agency's voting history of 3–2 splits along party lines. In theory, the FCC is an independent agency (ibid, p. 717). But in practice, political appointments to the agency's top leadership positions make the FCC extremely dependent on the president for determining the current policy environment and objectives. The back-and-forth party control from the oval office and capitol hill means that the FCC risks veering in one policy direction and then the other, unable to present a consistent regulatory environment for more than two presidential terms at a time.

Will the 2015 Open Internet Order be sacked in the wake of the current power shift? That question worries millions of Americans.

V. THE FUTURE OF BROADBAND EXPANSION.

1. A New Chairman. On December 15, Wheeler issued a brief statement about his resignation. It said nothing about his reasons for leaving, but it did clarify how Wheeler envisions the legacy he leaves behind: "a thriving communications sector, where robust investment and world-leading innovation continue to drive our economy and meaningful improvements in the lives of the American people" (FCC Statement, 2016).

The FCC's announcement gave his date of his departure as January 20, the date of President Trump's inauguration. "Following custom for an FCC chairman, Wheeler resigned his seat when the new administration of Donald Trump began on January 20, 2017", leaving the new President with a new Chairman to appoint (Cone, 2016). The normally five-person FCC panel began the Trump administration with a 2-1 Republican majority. The Senate did not outright deny the appointment of Jessica Rosenworcel, but it delayed her confirmation and went to recess. Rosenworcel's term ended more than two weeks before the inauguration (McMill, 2016).

Chairman Ajit Pai, always outspoken against net neutrality and the current Title II regime, will "need to be reconfirmed by the Senate before the end of [2017] because his current five-year term as a commissioner expires", but he requires no confirmation process to get started (Fiegerman, 2017). That leaves two vacancies on the FCC board to bring it to a full five. As only three can be from the same political party, we can most likely expect a split of three Republicans and two Democrats.

2. Subsidies. As the net neutrality movement says farewell to Chairman Wheeler, it must wonder about the fate of other programs Wheeler favored. These programs and policy developments were part of Wheeler's larger vision for the future, which included net neutrality as only one component in expanding high-speed broadband Internet to everyone in the U.S.

Will the political power shift bring an end to programs such as subsidized broadband for low-income homes, who could benefit from access to job applications, educational sites, and other social services? At the same meeting that set the FCC's new privacy rules for ISPs, the agency approved a plan for subsidizing broadband Internet access for low-income families (Kang, 31 Mar. 2016). "Those eligible for programs like the Supplemental Nutrition Assistance Program and tribal and veterans' benefits will be able to apply for the subsidy. The funds can be used for wireless or fixed-wire broadband" (ibid). The FCC's plan to fund the $2.25B project resembles methods it used on telcos to subsidize universal telephone service: line-item charges on wireless and Internet bills. The vote was approved 3–2, along partisan lines.

3. Municipal Broadband. Not all underserved areas lack the resources to take the broadband expansion into their own hands. Cities have found they can create their own municipal broadband service, effectively serve the entire community, and recoup their costs in about a decade. But the major ISPs have taken these proactive cities to court, and so far, the courts have not sided with the cities. Chairman Wheeler was a proponent of municipal broadband, and it is worth examining as a major component of the policy goal of expanding broadband nationwide.

Chanute, Kansas confronted the problem of broadband expansion without being at the mercy of cable companies or the FCC's complex subsidy schemes. Rather than wait for costly last-mile infrastructure to come to it, Chanute built its own (Lefler, 2014). The city projected it would take ten short years for their project to pay for itself, and this proactive approach is but one example of a growing wave of cities taking the broadband bull by the horns.

The overwhelming successes of hundreds of municipal broadband projects make it difficult to justify there being "legislative barriers to public-owned networks in 19 states" (Settles, 2014). "Over 400 public-owned networks operate in the United States, according to the Institute of Local Self-Reliance… covering business districts, industrial parks, and medical and university campuses" (ibid).

These projects are largely a success, with cities seeing increased service to outlying residential areas, increased employment, increased access to health care information and video-conference doctor visits, reduced government spending on broadband expenses, profits on the broadband service which are used to eliminate certain taxes, and higher speeds for everyone—all without needing to wait for the larger subsidized companies to get around to building infrastructure for the city (ibid).

On the same day as the voting on the 2015 Open Internet Order, the FCC voted 3–2 in favor of an order "seeking to pre-empt those state laws" which created "barriers to broadband investment" and specifically laws unfavorable to "municipalities" who wanted to build their own broadband networks in "areas of little or no service" (Reuters, 2016).

While municipal broadband fits in with Chairman Wheeler's vision of expanding broadband access, nineteen states have laws preventing its development, laws "often passed at the behest of private Internet service providers that didn't want to face competition" (Brodkin, 2015). On the forefront of the ensuing litigation stood Tennessee and North Carolina, each of which had limits on publicly created Internet service (Fung, 2015). Cities in those states asked the FCC to intervene and allow them to provide municipal broadband despite the state laws.

EPB, the municipal utility serving Chattanooga, TN, petitioned the FCC to allow it to deliver Internet to communities outside of the 600-square mile area they service (Settles, 20 Jul. 2014). Wilson, NC petitioned to provide Internet to local communities, and the FCC determined residents who lived outside the service range of utility companies in Chattanooga and Wilson had no broadband service at all (Gross, 2015).

The states challenged the FCC's interference, and the legal authority behind it. In August 2016, "the United States Court of Appeals for the Sixth Circuit upheld restrictive laws in North Carolina and Tennessee that will halt the growth of such networks" (Kang, 26 Aug. 2016). While the court agreed that municipal networks were valuable, it disagreed with the FCC's legal arguments on its power to pre-empt state laws (ibid). The court ruled the FCC could not block North Carolina and Tennessee "from setting limits on municipal broadband expansion" (Reuters, 2016).

Wheeler openly lamented a decision that "appears to halt the promise of jobs, investment, and opportunity that community broadband has provided" (ibid). Chairman Pai applauded the decision. "Rather than wasting its time on illegal efforts to intrude on the prerogatives of state governments, the FCC should focus on implementing a broadband deployment agenda to eliminate regulatory barriers that discourage those in the private sector from deploying and upgrading next-generation networks" (Qtd. in ibid).

Where private cable companies have powerful lobbies, such as in North Carolina, they can exert powerful influence over whether cities can develop their own broadband projects. While the FCC's Title II authority gives them some control over broadband companies, these companies can still use other political and legal channels to achieve aims which directly contravene the FCC's vision for robust, high-speed broadband for everyone.

VI. Conclusion: Happy Trails

1. Broadband Will Expand—but on Whose Terms? An analysis in the *University of Toledo Law Review* summarized the position of the broadband ISPs as for-profit companies faced with massive infrastructure costs who want the option to generate revenue through "price discrimination and content control" (Missirian, 2016, p. 347). And why not? Shouldn't the owners of an infrastructure get to do whatever they want with it?

This position, and arguments for a less neutral net, have little to do with longstanding realities of common-carrier policy, and even less to do with centuries of policy development on how the state regulates a natural monopoly. The ISPs now find themselves in a regulatory environment that more closely resembles the early days of the telephone, when AT&T was encouraged to build infrastructure to service the entire nation, but regulated in its ability to price the services.

The ISPs would like to prevent municipal broadband, and why wouldn't they? If cities take care of their own Internet infrastructure, the ISPs lose entire markets. If cities can generate public profits from serving nearby communities, who needs a private ISP?

In the near future, with the appointment of Chairman Pai, we are unlikely to see the FCC initiate any challenges to the states blocking municipal broadband in favor of cable industry lobbies. But it will be increasingly more painful to the residents of those states when they see their neighbors solving all the broadband problems themselves. Pressure from within the states may obviate the need for FCC involvement. Under Title II, we have the government regulating private companies which provide a service to the government. These private companies have a strong ally in Chairman Pai, but governments in every state will realize that municipalities can cut out the middlemen and be their own ISPs.

A robust network of municipalities with high-speed broadband, both wired and wireless, would be a boon to the public sector. Regulating that network according to a common-carrier philosophy is consistent with the idea of broadband as a public utility. Right now, public entities— cities—in some states remain subject to the expansion schedules of private companies.

2. The Influence of Political Appointees. In a more general sense, the power-shift-in-progress serves as a case study of the political appointee system. The risk of pulling the FCC back and forth on policy determinations with every presidential election is often suffered by agencies staffed by short-term appointees who have short-term goals.

Developing consistent long-term policies and seeing them implemented over several presidential administrations may not be possible. This is not a problem only for the FCC, but a system-wide problem in the federal government. I have covered its causes, effects, and possible solutions in my literature review *The Problems of Political Appointees in Federal Government.*

The future of the 2015 Open Internet Order remains in the hands of new set of commissioners, and a chairman who never liked the Order in the first place. Broadband expansion will continue, but it may come to us in a climate that favors a private sector approach over a public utility approach.

REFERENCES

Brodkin, Jon. (26 Feb. 2015). "FCC overturns state laws that protect ISPs from local competition: Municipal broadband networks could expand because of FCC's controversial vote." *ArsTechnica.* http://arstechnica.com/business/2015/02/fcc-overturns-state-laws-that-protect-isps-from-local-competition/

Brodkin, Jon. (14 Jun. 2016). "After net neutrality loss, ISPs get ready to take case to Supreme Court". *ArsTechnica*.com. https://arstechnica.com/tech-policy/2016/06/supreme-court-get-ready-isps-wont-give-up-net-neutrality-fight/

Cleland, Scott. (19 Jan. 2017). "FCC's net neutrality enforcement policy should be rated zero". *TheHill*.com. http://thehill.com/blogs/pundits-blog/technology/315089-fcc-democrats-get-a-zero-for-enforcing-net-neutrality

Coldewey, Devin. (11 Jan. 2017). "FCC voices 'serious concerns' over AT&T's zero-rating scheme". *TechCrunch*.com. https://techcrunch.com/2017/01/11/fcc-voices-serious-concerns-over-atts-zero-rating-scheme/

Cone, Allen. (15 Dec. 2016). "FCC Chairman Tom Wheeler to resign". *United Press International. UPI*.com http://www.upi.com/Top_News/US/2016/12/15/FCC-Chairman-Tom-Wheeler-to-resign/5711481819346/

FCC (Federal Communications Commission). (9 Jul. 2015). Order DA 15-776, "In the Matter of TerraCom, Inc., and YourTel America, Inc." *FCC*.gov. https://apps.fcc.gov/edocs_public/attachmatch/DA-15-776A1_Rcd.pdf

FCC. (5 Nov. 2015). Order DA 15-1241, "In the Matter of Cox Communications, Inc." *FCC*.gov. https://apps.fcc.gov/edocs_public/attachmatch/DA-15-1241A1_Rcd.pdf

FCC Statement. (15 Dec. 2016). "Chairman Wheeler Announces His Plans to Step Down". *FCC*.gov. https://apps.fcc.gov/edocs_public/attachmatch/DOC-342617A1.pdf

Fiegerman, Seth. (24 Jan. 2017). "President trump has found his man to regulate the media". *CNN Tech*. *CNN*.com. http://money.cnn.com/2017/01/23/technology/trump-fcc-chairman/

Friedlander, Simone A. (2016). "Net Neutrality and the FCC's 2015 Open Internet Order." *Berkeley Technology Law Journal*, Special Issue, Vol. 31: 905-929. DOI: 10.15779/Z382S0F.

Fung, Brian. (9 Nov. 2015). Obama championed cheap, fast, city-run Internet. His administration won't." *The Washington Post*. https://www.washingtonpost.com/news/the-switch/wp/2015/11/09/the-fccs-intervention-on-city-run-broadband-may-be-in-trouble/

Fung, Brian. (15 Jun. 2016). "The net neutrality court
decision, in plain English". *The Washington Post.
WashingtonPost*.com.
https://www.washingtonpost.com/news/the-
switch/wp/2016/06/15/the-net-neutrality-court-
decision-in-plain-english/

Gross, Grant. (26 Feb. 2015). "FCC votes to overturn state
laws limiting municipal broadband". *IDG
Communications, Inc. CIO*.com.
http://www.cio.com/article/2889633/fcc-votes-to-
overturn-state-laws-limiting-municipal-
broadband.html

Howell, Bronwyn. (22 Jan. 2016). "The hypocrisy of the
anti-paid prioritization movement".
TechPolicyDaily.com.
http://www.techpolicydaily.com/internet/the-
hypocrisy-of-the-anti-paid-prioritization-movement/

Kan, Stephanie. (Symposium 2016). "Split Net Neutrality:
Applying Traditional First Amendment Protections to
the Modern Interweb." *Houston Law Review, 53*(4):
1149-1177.

Kang, Cecilia. (7 Mar. 2016). "Verizon Settles With F.C.C.
Over Hidden Tracking via 'Supercookies'".
NYTimes.com.
https://www.nytimes.com/2016/06/15/technology/net-
neutrality-fcc-appeals-court-ruling.html

Kang, Cecelia. (31 Mar. 2016). "F.C.C. Approves Broadband
Subsidy for Low-Income Households". *Technology, The
New York Times. NYTimes*.com.

https://www.nytimes.com/2016/04/01/technology/fcc-approves-broadband-subsidy-for-low-income-households.html

Kang, Cecilia. (14 Jun. 2016). "Court Backs Rules Treating Internet as Utility, Not Luxury". *NYTimes*.com. https://www.nytimes.com/2016/06/15/technology/net-neutrality-fcc-appeals-court-ruling.html

Kang, Cecelia. (26 Aug. 2016). "Broadband Law Could Force Rural Residents Off Information Superhighway". *Technology, The New York Times. NYTimes*.com. https://www.nytimes.com/2016/08/29/technology/broadband-law-could-force-rural-residents-off-information-superhighway.html

Kang, Cecilia. (27 Oct. 2016). "Broadband Providers Will Need Permission to Collect Private Data". *Technology, The New York Times. NYTimes*.com. https://www.nytimes.com/2016/10/28/technology/fcc-tightens-privacy-rules-for-broadband-providers.html

Lefler, Dion. (24 May 2014). "Chanute aims to provide speedy Internet service to all homes, businesses in town." *Wichita Eagle*. Retrieved from http://www.kansas.com/news/article1144149.html

Lyons, Daniel A. (2015). "Innovations in Mobile Broadband Pricing." *Denver University Law Review*, 92(3): 453-492.

McMill, Margaret H., and Byers, Alex. (15 Dec. 2016). "FCC Chairman Tom Wheeler to resign". *Politico*.com. http://www.politico.com/story/2016/12/fcc-chairman-tom-wheeler-to-resign-232676

Missirian, David E. (Winter, 2016). "Net Neutrality: The Information Highway Which Only the Wealthy Few Will Be Allowed to Travel." *University of Toledo Law Review*, 47(2): 327-348.

Reuters. (10 Aug. 2016). "U.S. Court Blocks FCC Bid to Expand Public Broadband". *Technology, The New York Times. NYTimes*.com. https://www.nytimes.com/2016/08/10/technology/10reuters-usa-internet-ruling.html

Settles, Craig. (20 Jul. 2014). "Mr. Wheeler, tear down these walls: The economic case for removing barriers to muni broadband". *GigaOm*.com. https://gigaom.com/2014/07/20/mr-wheeler-tear-down-these-walls-the-economic-case-for-removing-barriers-to-muni-broadband/

Settles, Craig. (27 Jul. 2014). "States, stand down! Let community broadband innovate". *GigaOm*.com. https://gigaom.com/2014/07/27/states-stand-down-let-community-broadband-innovate/

Singer, Natasha. (24 Nov. 2015). "Jonathan Mayer, Well-Known Online Security Expert, Joins F.C.C.". *The New York Times, NYTimes*.com. https://bits.blogs.nytimes.com/2015/11/24/jonathan-mayer-well-known-online-security-expert-joins-f-c-c/

US States Court of Appeals for the District of Columbia Circuit. (14 Jun. 2016). No. 15-1063. *United States Telecom Association v. FCC*. https://www.cadc.uscourts.gov/internet/opinions.nsf/3F95E49183E6F8AF85257FD200505A3A/$file/15-1063-1619173.pdf

Watts, Kathryn A. "Controlling Presidential Control." *Michigan Law Review*, 114(5): 683-745.

WSGR (Wilson Sonsini Goodrich & Rosati). (10 Dec. 2015). "Five Things to Know About Net Neutrality". *WSGR*.com. https://www.wsgr.com/WSGR/Display.aspx?SectionName=publications/PDFSearch/wsgralert-net-neutrality.htm

www.ingramcontent.com/pod-product-compliance
Lightning Source LLC
Chambersburg PA
CBHW060632280326
41933CB00012B/2008